Twin Adventures From A Simpler Time: A Memoir

I0438011

Twin Adventures From A Simpler Time: A Memoir

Dotty Cronan

iUniverse, Inc.
New York   Bloomington

Twin Adventures From A Simpler Time: A Memoir

Copyright © 2009 by Dotty Cronan

iUniverse books may be ordered through booksellers or by contacting:

iUniverse
1663 Liberty Drive
Bloomington, IN 47403
www.iuniverse.com
1-800-Authors (1-800-288-4677)

ISBN: 978-1-4401-6690-7 (sc)
ISBN: 978-1-4401-6691-4 (ebook)

Printed in the United States of America

iUniverse rev. date: 10/15/2009

Acknowledgements

Thank you to my twin brother, Charlie/Chuck, for giving me an adventurous start in life, and our continuous connection. Thank you to my husband, Carl, for his constant love and support throughout this process and our entire marriage. Many thanks to my son, Dave, for his patience and technical help involved in the process of book publishing. Thank you to my oldest son, Drew, his wife Juli, and their daughter Emily for their encouragement. Dan, my third son, is much appreciated for helping me to laugh when I wanted to scream. I am grateful to the Barnegat Writers Group for their helpful critiques, especially Nancy Gallagher, its founder and leader.

Contents

A Rough Start

My tiny fingers throbbed, as I clung to the chain link fence, yelling through it, "Mommy, don't leave us! Please don't leave us!" As Mom's petite frame walked away, getting smaller and smaller until she disappeared like a windswept bubble, my twin brother pried my hands from the wire and led me to the sandbox. We perched on its edge like two frightened canaries. Puffing himself up, Charlie put an arm around my trembling shoulders and pointed out the fascinating items within the cage-like enclosure: rope swings with wooden seats, gray metal seesaws, red wagons, pastel beach balls and brightly painted tin pails lying in the sand.

"Dot, your face looks like a waffle iron from crushing into that fence," Charlie said with a quivering smile. Then he reached into the pocket of my yellow jacket and pulled out the lace-trimmed handkerchief Mom had tucked there "just in case." He dabbed at my tears and assured me, "Mom will come back for us, I promise." From the safety of his arms, I peeked at our surroundings and discovered a playground full of solitary boys and girls looking even more devastated than the pair of us. We had each other.

"Welcome to your first day of kindergarten," called Sister Mary Claire from the steps of the blue and white house as she clanged her big brass bell. Her black veils filled with air as her arm swung up and down. My first giggle of the day burst forth when Charlie referred to the nun as a "puffy penguin."

"Ah, so you're the Merlau twins," said Sister, as Charlie and I slid through the big blue doorway. "Charles, it looks like you've got a couple of inches on your sister already. And let's see … darker hair and blue eyes in a handsome face."

"Dorothy, if you will raise your eyes to me, I'll be able to see what color they are." Reluctantly turning my moist eyes up to the flowing creature in front of me, I heard the most amazing words: "My oh my, they are like beautiful chestnuts in an angel's face, surrounded by halo-colored hair."

Wow, maybe this place isn't so bad after all.

At Holy Name School in East Orange, New Jersey in the 1940's, the kindergarten was located in the old converted convent next to the brick building that housed the first to eighth graders. The Sisters of Charity lived in the new convent around the corner next to the church on Dodd Street.

The interior of the kindergarten was even more fascinating than the exterior and play-yard. We stared in awe at the huge, shiny blackboards hung on lime green walls. The overflowing bookshelves dazzled us. At home we had one book, a hand-me-down copy of bible stories. Rainbows of Crayola crayons, fanned out on each of the small round tables, begged to be picked up. They felt like little magic wands in our hands. At home we shared a package of eight crayons. The multi-colored construction paper, spread across the center of each table, resembled Joseph's coat of many colors. There was no construction paper at home; things were tight during World War II.

This place was definitely not so bad.

Choosing one of the low colorful tables presented no problem; we headed for the two empty seats at the yellow table with six green chairs, the colors of summer. I blinked away the last tear of the day when Charlie pulled his chair close to mine and praised my "brave" behavior. My ex-womb-mate, who is two hours and thirty-three minutes younger than I, was establishing his role as my "big brother" twin.

Multiple Twins

Two days into kindergarten, I landed on my knees hollering to my brother, "Jerry knocked me off the swing!"

"I'll take care of it," said Charlie, as he rushed to the swing set. After some boisterous words and minor shoving, the Merlau vs. Burke bout ended. I marched to the swing of my choice, stretched my short arms up along the long ropes and pulled myself upward and plopped myself down like a Duncan yo-yo. My hero wiped his hands together and returned to his game of marbles. Before I could pump my swing to its full potential, I spotted Jerry and another kid strutting towards Charlie. Dragging my Buster Browns in the dirt to stop the swing, I jumped off and ran to my brother's side just in time to hear Jerry introduce *his* twin brother to *my* twin brother. Ooops, Marty Burke towered over Charlie.

Clang, clang, clang – saved by the bell. Apparently, Sister Mary Claire had witnessed round one and retrieved her bell from inside, putting a stop to round two before it could get underway. She declared it a draw and instructed the contestants to get along with each other, "Or else."

That's when the four of us learned the power of "Sister said." Whenever we came within striking distance of each other, we all shouted, "Sister said" and scurried off in different directions.

By the end of kindergarten, Charlie and I realized there were more than the Merlau, Burke, and Bobbsey twins in the world. We learned that Holy Name boasted at least a dozen pair of twins and that the Burkes and we belonged to a special group. Remaining mad at members of the same club became quite difficult.

Each spring, the photographer with the long, bushy mustache scrambled into the auditorium with his big box camera, a black tripod, and a cloak to throw over himself and his camera. He resembled Felix the Cat digging into his bag of tricks.

Every year, the twins of Holy Name waited, as if for Santa, for the newspaper containing their group picture. As soon as Charlie and I located ourselves in the picture, we'd scan the photo for our friends, Jerry and Marty.

Puddles and Punishments

"How did you two get so soaked?" asked Sister Alice, our first grade teacher, her dainty hands upon her somewhere hips, somewhere under her billowing habit. She pleaded for an answer through the hazel eyes in her square face, surrounded by protruding, starched, white linen, and flowing black veils.

"We're sorry, Sister, we were just breaking ice off a puddle," I said, as Charlie, standing just beyond Sister's blinders, pretended to stomp puddles like the numerous ones we had smashed on our mile-long walk to school. Literally one mile of tree-lined streets to school, one mile home for lunch, another one back to school, and, finally, the best one at three o'clock. No wonder we were so slim. Charlie kept up his pantomime until he'd accomplished his goal -- getting me to giggle.

"I know what you're up to, young man," said Sister Alice as she turned to the comedian behind her. "And, I know it took more than one puddle to get *that* saturated and be *this* late for school." After dragging Charlie next to me, where she could keep an eye on both of "the impossible twins," she straightened her picture-frame headdress and glared at us. "Get those socks and shoes off, put them on the radiator, and pull up chairs for yourselves."

Our "punishment" was to remain in the classroom by ourselves next to the nice warm radiator, while our classmates joined the rest of the student body in the chilly auditorium to see a Mary movie. Our long walk, that fall day, had provided oodles of icy puddles just waiting to be shattered. So we spent our incarceration reenacting each and every puddle-smashing episode, leaping like frogs, our bare feet slapping the hardwood floor. When we ran out of stories and our socks had dried, we spent the rest of our internment playing with our sock puppets. They gobbled up the contents of Sister's desk: the little cricket-sounding clicker, a black leather catechism, boxes of white chalk, blackboard erasers, and, of course, the infamous wooden ruler.

With the approach of our classmates, headed up by Sister Alice, our puppets stopped eating and scurried onto our feet followed by dry shoes. Replacing the smirks on our faces with sorrowful frowns, we presented ourselves as such contrite delinquents that Sister gave each of us the same holy picture and box of candy the good boys and girls had received.

Since Sister had said, "Don't eat your candy until you've had your lunch," we each pretended to feed our candy to our three-inch Lady of Fatima picture on our way home. When Mom greeted us at the door of our green and white, two-story house, we explained the empty boxes by saying, "Our Lady ate them." Hey, we had gotten away with blaming missing cookies on our Raggedy Ann and Andy dolls for years. But on that particular day, Mom decided the pretend-game was up and calmly replied, "I guess Mary ate your lunch too," as she cleared the table of our Yoo-Hoos and peanut butter sandwiches. We marched back to school to the tune of our growling stomachs.

Trapeze Artists

Although our father was a stern disciplinarian and never heard of gentle persuasion, he showed his love by fixing or building things. One of his prize projects was a big, sturdy set of trapeze bars constructed with wooden planks, long bolts, steel chains and lead crossbars. One end of our trapeze set measured about six feet in length and maybe five feet high. That section consisted of stanchions and one long, stationary, lead pipe, on which Charlie and I could bend our legs and hang by the back of our knees or by our hands alongside of each other while planning our stunts for the swinging high bar at the other end. The high-bar portion of the frame measured about ten feet high and five feet wide, with long chains hanging approximately three feet apart from the top beam. Attached to both ends of a three-foot pipe were spring clips that could be attached to the chains at any height we chose.

To perform the greatest trapeze act ever, Charlie climbed the built-in ladder of the taller section, and clipped the metal bar to the chains, a couple of feet below the top frame. He proceeded to hang by his knees, holding another lead pipe horizontally in his hands, while I clamored onto that bar and hung by my knees. Double-decker trapeze twins!

Since this stunt called for an assistant, Jean, our older sister, grabbed my hands, backed up as far as she could, and let go. Her release sent us swinging back and forth, like a couple of monkeys. Her next role was to play the part of the audience and applaud, her status of big sister having been honed over years of supervising us. She praised and cheered our accomplishments with more enthusiasm than a high school cheerleader.

One day, Jean and I were watching Charlie performing all sorts of contortions on the long, lower bar. His antics would have put a ferret to shame, until Jean came up with a series of requests: "Hang by your hands and knees, now let go with one hand, now let go with the other hand, now let go with one leg." Charlie hung by one knee for a split second before falling to the ground. Boy was he mad … and embarrassed in front of his audience.

On a different day, I embarrassed myself in front of, well, no one. Planning on swinging into the clouds, I had lowered the bar to a position I judged to be just above my head, backed up, extended my arms in front of me, and ran straight for the bar.

BAM! I ran smack into the lead pipe; my hands passed just under it … my head did not. I crashed to the ground as if hit by a baseball bat. I'm not sure how long I lay there, since no one was around to help me. But after shaking my groggy head and touching the huge lump on my forehead, I immediately looked around to see if anyone had witnessed my stupidity. I couldn't have felt more embarrassed if I had been caught naked in front of a thousand Sisters of Charity. A trapeze artist is not supposed to make such a dumb mistake. I staggered into the house and up to my bedroom where I hung my aching head in shame for the duration of the long, hot, summer afternoon.

When I finally heard Mom's voice calling all over the house for me, I forced myself to trudge down to the dinner table. Even Mom's famous meatloaf didn't perk me up; I just wanted the day to be over. But that wish was not to be granted, anymore than my budding career.

"Honey, where did you get that bump?" Mom asked.

"What bump?"

"The one bulging across your entire forehead."

"Oh, that … I don't know."

"Come on now, you must know. Did you hit your head on something?"

"I don't know."

After the longest game of Twenty Questions ever played by our family, I was still answering, "I don't know."

It turned out that running into the trapeze bar was not the dumbest thing I did that day. I was not suffering from amnesia; I was suffering from gross embarrassment. My repeated refusal to tell what had happened led to an interrogation at the hands of my impatient father.

I might still be getting the strap on my bottom if Mom hadn't intervened with her gentle approach. "Honey, you're upsetting the entire family. Don't be embarrassed, just tell me what happened."

I'm not sure if I really cared more about "the entire family" than my own butt, but the floodgates opened and spilled out my guts. Mom's hugs, kisses, and reassurance that I was not stupid revived my dreams of becoming half of the world's greatest trapeze twins.

Halloween Tragedies

My first Trick-or-Treat trek, at age six, was a terrifying evening of goblins, ghosts, and witches stirring up a wicked brew of fear. Charlie took it all in stride and kept whispering to me, "They're only costumes, like the clown outfit you have on and the tramp clothes I'm wearing."

Charlie grasped one of my hands, and Jean held the other while repeating a litany of praise. "Just one more house, you can do it, you're a brave little clown. Just one more house, you can do it...." she chanted with each tug-o-war step through the neighborhood. The post-Halloween nightmares lasted much longer than the candy.

In preparation for my second Halloween outing, Mom started acting excited a month in advance. "Halloween is coming soon, so let's think up some ideas for costumes. You could be Little Bo Peep and wear the beautiful pink flowered dress Aunt Bert made you for kindergarten graduation." It took two weeks for Mom to talk me into preparing for another Halloween.

The adventure of having my aunt, who had her own seamstress business, fussing over me while altering my long dress, kept my mind off Halloween monsters. She lengthened it by adding another row of ruffles and fashioned a wonderful floppy hat of the same fabric. I spun around her bridal shop, pretending to be one of the beautiful brides in her window, especially the one in the three-tier lace gown. When the dreaded night arrived, Mom proclaimed, "Charlie is the greatest pirate ever," and, "Little Bo Peep has nothing to fear from scary costumes filled with harmless children. This year will be fun!"

Wrong! It was an encore of the previous year's tragedy: Jean and Charlie tugging me along while struggling to hold the three expanding bags of loot. Loot, by the way, that I had no qualms about devouring ... witches brew or not. But, once again, nightmares outlasted the candy.

The next year, Mom tried a different tactic. Before the leaves fell off the trees, she took me to Woolworth's Five & Dime and had me pick out the scariest monster mask I could find. She waited patiently while I examined every mask from every angle, gingerly touched and turned each one, and finally played peek-a-boo with a chosen few in the cracked mirror on the counter. In the end, I chose the most fearsome one of all.

It was a plastic, dish-like thing with a stretchy string that went around the back of my head. It looked like a green blob and was creepy enough for me. I had two whole weeks to practice scaring my family with my mask. When Halloween arrived, I ran gleefully around the neighborhood, racing up and down front steps, yelling "Boo!" at every door. That year, Charlie and Jean had a hard time keeping up with the little monster ahead of them.

To celebrate my success, Mom agreed to let me go with Charlie to the first "Haunted House" being held in the basement of our next-door neighbor. Eddie Robinson and his teenage friends had been preparing for this fearsome event during the weeks I had been preparing to be fearless. With a nickel for admission in one hand and a candy bar in the other, we skipped through the opening in the hedges.

In those days, basements in my neighborhood were not finished with paneled walls and decorated with comfortable furniture; they had dirt floors, cobwebs on the cracked windows, and coal and soot around the furnace. They were lit by a series of ceiling light bulbs with hanging pull-strings. But on this evening, as we descended the stairs, the only light we could make out was the glow of the huge furnace and one tiny night-light at the far end of the cellar. Once the door was slammed shut behind us, bloody, dirty creatures started jumping out of dark corners like trolls from under a bridge. They came screaming out of the coal bin, swinging porous bags of soot in our faces, and knocking us down on dirty mattresses strewn on the floor. Then they vanished into the shadows. We lay trembling, trying to figure a way out before the next attack. As we crawled along the floor, stringy cobwebs slid over our faces. There was no way out, except to feel our way along the maze of low, temporary, blood-red, plywood walls that concealed the monsters -- monsters with scarred faces and humps on their backs. Invisible monsters that whispered, cackled, and shrieked at us.

Despite the efforts of my loving family, the Haunted House experience sent my fear of Halloween right back to square one.

The next year it was: "Just one more house, you can do it…" all over again.

Turkey, Canaries, and Parakeets

All of our childhood Thanksgivings were spent at the home of Aunt Bert and Uncle Jim, Mom's oldest brother and a Newark police officer. He was round and jolly, and Aunt Bert resembled the pictures of Kate Smith on Mom's record albums. My aunt was a big woman with a big heart. She also had a bum leg from an automobile accident, but never let it interfere with her many activities or wardrobe of flowing dresses. Although their home lacked kids, it was not lacking in love; they showered it on each other, on their numerous pets, and Jean, Charlie, and me. Uncle John, the middle of Mom's three brothers, a bachelor and war veteran, and our Grandma Feeney were always part of the festivities.

After all the hugs and kisses at the front door each Thanksgiving, we spent at least half an hour playing with Aunt Bert and Uncle Jim's family of dogs. The canine family consisted of five funny little brown and tan creatures called Miniature Manchester Terriers. Charlie and I always joked about expecting their bulging eyes to pop out of their tiny heads. The dogs had pointy ears and snouts, which made them appear very alert. They were, in fact, always ready to fetch the rubber balls we tossed.

Each year, the momma dog got crabbier, but her "puppies" were always playful. Our favorite was a big fellow, twice the size of the others, who looked the most like a real dog. Aunt Bert explained that Buddy was a throwback and should have been destroyed, but they loved him too much.

After romping with the dogs for a while, Charlie and I became very aware of the tantalizing aroma coming from the kitchen. We were drawn to the oven for a peek at the most delicious thing in the warm kitchen -- the big, fat, juicy turkey.

While thinking about the roasting bird, we moved on to the room full of singing, talking birds. The canaries ranged in color from pale yellow to bright orange, some were yellow and black and others orange and brown. Sometimes the drabbest ones were the best singers.

One particular Thanksgiving, when I was about seven, I thought about the canary Aunt Bert had given Mom a couple of years before; it had been as yellow as daffodils and sang like an angel. Early that fall, I had found Mom sitting at the bottom of our back hall stairway, cradling her dead canary in her trembling hands, while trying to wipe her tears on the shoulder of her print housedress. I suddenly felt as sad in Aunt Bert's bird room as I had that day in the back hall. When Charlie noticed me gazing sadly at a canary that resembled the one Mom had lost, he whispered in my ear, "Aunt Bert will give Mom a new one." I knew he was right.

We moved on to the hyperactive finches with their constant fluttering and chattering and their brilliant orange and gray feathers. Feeling better, I visited my favorites: the talking parakeets that said things like "pretty boy," "hello," and "good-bye," just like Sunny Boy at home. Aunt Bert had gifted Charlie and me with the beautiful green bird the same year Mom had received her canary. I felt another pang of sadness and tried to think of all the things we had to be thankful for. With Charlie by my side, we said good-bye to the lively little birds in the cages and moved on to the big bird in the oven.

Every year, as my brother and I sat next to each other staring at the abundant spread of food on the table, the dogs stared at us, as if expecting our eyes to pop out. We piled plump olives, crispy celery stuffed with cream cheese, and slices of shimmering cranberry sauce onto our plates. Next we'd add mountains of stuffing and a pile of fluffy mashed potatoes, into which we gouged craters to hold lakes of brown gravy.

The last piece of food we added to our overflowing plates was always our choice of the golden-brown turkey parts. Everyone waited in great expectation as "the twins" chose the drumsticks, as we did every year.

Halfway through the meal, when we realized our bulging eyes were definitely bigger then our little tummies, Mom would frown at our half empty plates and say, "Come on now, finish all your food." Wasting food was not allowed at home, and desserts were not served to food-wasters while children were "starving in other countries." But we were at Aunt Bert's home, and year after year she came to our rescue, announcing, "The dogs are waiting for the leftovers."

When the others had finally finished their dinners, and the desserts were served, we gloated over our victory while filling our faces with spicy-smelling pumpkin pie smothered in whipped cream.

Bunnies, Ducks, and Uncle John

After our annual hunt for the hidden Easter baskets full of candy, which we were prohibited from eating until after mass when our fast could be broken, Dad, who was Protestant, dropped his Catholic family off at church, went back home, then picked us up an hour later. Like many women those days, Mom didn't drive. Once we kids had consumed our oatmeal, we were finally allowed to dig into the contents of our baskets: colored hard-boiled eggs, Peeps marshmallow chicks, jelly beans in oodles of hues and flavors, and one, big, solid chocolate bunny each. Jean had a dark brown basket; Charlie and I had matching yellow ones.

While the ham boiled and then baked, Jean helped Mom peel, slice, and boil potatoes and carrots, and Charlie and I set the dining room table for nine. The first challenging part of our task was removing the bulky cloth folder of silverware from the buffet drawer. We placed it in the center of one end of the table and carefully opened each side, until it lay flat on the table. Then we gingerly removed the straight pins that held the protective, orange fabric over the sterling silver, which may or may not need polishing -- with that pink, smelly stuff -- once uncovered. As we unveiled the silverware, our apprehension changed to woe or delight depending on the condition of the silver.

Early afternoon doorbell-ringing announced the arrivals of Aunt Bert and Uncle Jim, then Grandma and Uncle John, who lived together. One year, Uncle John was accompanied by a real live Easter bunny, "For the three kids." Jean named the white, fluffy rabbit, Suzie. We loved feeling her pink nose on the palm of our hand as she nibbled at slivers of carrot. Another year, Uncle John surprised "the twins" with two yellow baby ducks we named Gus and Zeke. All these lively, furry or feathered gifts filled us with joy, as did the ones made of paper or sugar.

Greeting cards the size of coloring books, decorated with velvet Easter bunnies, fuzzy chicks, and happy children, were among the surprises to be drawn from behind Uncle John's back. Each card contained enchanting messages about the love of an uncle for his niece or nephew. The feeling of love was definitely a two-way street. Other delightful treats to appear -- as if by magic -- were festively wrapped boxes containing the most delightful Easter eggs imaginable. Sometimes these ostrich-size eggs were made of chocolate and other times of white sugar; both were decorated with swirls of pink, blue, and yellow icing.

The tips of the smaller ends of the hollow eggs were cut off, leaving an opening approximately one inch in diameter. Pressing one eye to the opening, as with a telescope, we beheld another world: a miniature world of bunnies, barnyard animals, and children at play. Everything was made of sweet, edible candy, so tempting to eat, but so beautiful to just behold. The life span of these special eggs far surpassed that of our chocolate bunnies that were usually decapitated by Monday. The thoughtful gifts from Uncle John have remained in my memory as among the most charming I've ever received.

Judging by the smile on the face of our special uncle, I would say that time spent with Charlie and me ranked very high on his list of happy moments. Over the years, we came to realize that his happy-list was incredibly short.

One of the best gifts he ever presented us with was the story he told about one of the other janitors at the school where he worked. Uncle John had walked into the boiler room one day and found the kittens he had been feeding soaked with gasoline and his co-worker about to strike a match. "He was going to burn the poor little things," Uncle John said, with tears brimming in his eyes. "So I punched him in the nose." That day, he became an even bigger hero to us than when he came home from the war.

My first memory of Uncle John is one of a very handsome, solemn, thin man with dark eyes under thick black eyebrows, stepping slowly through the kitchen door of the flat he was to share with his mother, my Grandma Feeney. He was dressed in a khaki army uniform and a long, narrow hat that looked like an envelope tilted to one side of his head. We all yelled, "Surprise!" and threw confetti at him at his welcome-home party. He ate only a small piece of cake before retiring to the front parlor to stare out the window, a behavior that became standard. That's all I remember of Uncle John's welcome-home party.

All our happy times with Uncle John could be counted in moments. They lasted only as long as it took us to open and thrill over our unique presents and enjoy a holiday meal. Then Uncle John would be the first to leave. Someone else always drove Grandma home. It took us many years to realize he was heading home to his bottle ... as his father had done.

During our teenage years, Uncle John gifted us with an Aunt Violet. She adored him and put a smile on his face -- for a couple of years -- before leaving him. A few years later, Mom found her brother's body surrounded by empty bottles on the floor of his filthy flat. It breaks my heart to this day to think of the lifetime of battles he fought ... and lost.

The Right Side of the Tracks

On one side of the tracks sat a small dreary old shack. Cracked gray shingles clung to the outside; thick, gray soot coated the inside. A plump, gray-haired lady sat within, protected from the elements -- until the train whistle blew. The sound of the iron monster sprung her from her shed like a coo-coo bird from its' clock. She scurried to the gate, wrapped her calloused hands around the metal handle, and cranked away. The long wooden guardrail descended slowly across Myrtle Street, and the occasional automobile would roll safely to a stop moments before the speeding train roared past.

We enjoyed chatting with the old woman as she slowly turned the crank to raise the guardrail back to its vertical position -- until the next train came along. We loved visiting with her inside the little shack, especially on cold winter days. The pot-bellied stove warmed the pot-bellied lady and her two guests. She crammed herself into her square, wooden chair and we huddled on the rectangular footstool. Two plump, gnarled hands, and four small, flawless hands stretched toward the red-hot coals glowing inside the open stove. When we all stopped shivering, our friend would close the stove door to "preserve the heat, you know" and lean back in her chair. My brother and I leaned against each other, like bookends, ready for another fireside chat.

What we talked about, I do not remember. What our old friend's name was, I, sadly, do not remember. What I do remember is the warmth inside that little shack: winter, spring, summer or fall.

On the other side of the tracks, on summer days, Charlie and I waited with all the neighborhood children for the mid-day freight train. As the sun rose higher in the sky, anticipation climbed among the flock of kids. The sound of the distant whistle called the gaggle into formation -- a straight line along the tracks. The sight of the smoking train instigated a rowdy jostling for position, with the biggest kids naturally gaining the head of the line. But as the train passed by, the engineer always had enough lollypops to toss to every single child scurrying along the tracks. It was like Christmas in July, complete with a jolly, bearded, fat man.

So, you see, no matter what side of the tracks we were on, we were always on the right side of the tracks.

Mysterious Green "Things"

Kids were not as closely supervised in those days. Besides our long walks back and forth to school going unsupervised, our after-school activities were also left pretty much up to us. On our way home, we often stopped at the halfway point and wandered off Dodd Street into our end of Watsessing Park. The other half of the park extended all the way into the next town of Bloomfield. Arriving home anywhere between 3:20 and dinnertime constituted perfectly acceptable behavior as long as our uniforms remained clean. I really don't know if there were fewer predators, or if it was the lack of media coverage, but the minimal parental warning about not talking to strangers seemed to suffice.

In the park, some of the older kids stood around in cigarette-smoking circles, while some eighth grade couples sat on benches kissing. We declared both groups "yucky." Charlie and I usually played on the slides and swings with the other small-fry, except for one unfortunate day.

We strayed into a wooded area and discovered big green "things," the size of softballs, strewn on the ground beneath a huge tree. After staring at the mysterious objects and wondering if they had fallen from the tree, we picked them up and bounced them in our hands, amazed at their hefty weight. Some had already broken and spilled their sweet-smelling green guts on the ground. To this day, I don't know what the things were, some sort of fruit or gigantic nuts. What I do know is that we just had to discover if more of them were hidden up in the thick branches. Charlie shimmied up the trunk, like Jack up the beanstalk, and disappeared into the leafy branches while I waited patiently below for news of the mysterious green things.

"Dotty, there's tons of them up here. Stand back, I'm gonna drop some." Splat, splat, they landed, one after another, like bombs. The sturdy ones bounced and rolled but stayed intact.

"Stop a minute!" I shouted, "I wanna catch one."

"Okay. I'll climb down a little closer where you can see me dropping it."

Charlie lowered himself into view, reached up into the leaves, pulled one off a branch, and let it drop. I swear I can remember it cascading down, as if in slow motion. I can still see the big green thing plopping into my waiting hands and splitting open. I stared in horror as dozens of angry insects soared out and swarmed around my hands and arms. Shocked, I froze, as they continued to swarm and multiply to hundreds around my entire body. Of all the green things, I had to choose the same one as the bees. I snapped out of my trance when they started stinging.

"Help! Help!" I wailed as I threw the exploding bomb and ran. My friend Annette came running from the swings as Charlie slid down the tree and did an immediate evaluation of the damage. The attack-bees had stung my arms, face, and legs. Before flying away, they had even managed to squeeze through the sides of my Mary Janes and sting the bottoms of my feet, rendering me incapable of walking. I felt like I was full of flaming hot needles. Charlie sent Annette scampering to our house to fetch his wagon while he stayed with me. As we waited for her return, Charlie comforted me with words and hugs. The little red wagon became a little red ambulance when he helped me into it and sped home. His legs moved like those of a high school sprinter.

As Charlie panted and I sobbed, we managed to explain the whole encounter to our distraught mom. She was so preoccupied covering me with calamine lotion and kisses; she never said a word about the smelly, green gook smeared all over my gray and blue plaid uniform.

Horse Tales

One of the best things about our very early childhood summers was having more time to feed the horses. Since the horses whinnied twice as loud whenever we approached, we imagined they were saying, "Twice as many sugar cubes from the twins."

I'm not talking rodeo, jumper, or racehorse here; I'm talking rag, ice, and milk. The ragman's horse had a brown, skinny body with black legs, face, and tail under a layer of dirt; his coat was as drab as the rags in the cart he struggled to pull. We called him Dusty. He received twice as many Domino sugar cubes from us as the other, more robust, workhorses in the neighborhood.

The iceman's horse was not as memorable as old Dusty because we were more interested in receiving *our* treats. Crystal clear, dripping slivers of ice were delivered into our small hands from the enormous hands of Hank before he lugged the huge chunk of ice to Mom's icebox. The slivers were created each time his gigantic tongs slammed into both sides of a square foot of frozen water -- to grip, lift, and carry. We received the by-products with no less enthusiasm than today's kids reach for Rita's Italian Ice.

Snowy, the milkman's horse, was the most spectacular of all. His shiny coat matched the milk in the clear glass bottles and the white wagon he pulled. We shivered each time he stretched his massive neck to our outstretched hands -- palms up, fingers flat -- to receive the sweet, white cubes we offered. His squishy, slobbery lips swept our hands like a soft brush as the sugar disappeared. The thrill we received from this gentle giant rivaled the excitement of the local amusement park.

That reminds me of the first real lie I remember telling. It happened at the biggest amusement park in our area, Olympic Park in Irvington. Every summer, at least twice, Mom took Charlie and me on the bus to Newark, past the enticing smell of bread from Wards Bakery, to Grandma Feeney's house on Bergen Street. Grandma was a French-Canadian who wore her gray hair in a long braid down her long, straight back. She used to tell us of the games she played with the Indian children, one of her favorites involved rolling a wooden hoop with a stick. She told her stories with such enthusiasm and fondness that I used to imagine she, herself, was an Indian.

Grandma moved to the United States and married an Irishman we never got to meet because she had gathered her four children and left him and his empty bottles when my mother was young … but not young enough to forget the father she loved. She remembered he was an A-1 auto mechanic with jet-black hair and a dazzling smile. Mom also remembered he was kind to her, but fought bitterly with her mom. He became such a drinker he could no longer hold a job. Grandma went to work to raise the four kids on her own and never complained.

From Bergen Street, the four of us jumped on another bus to Olympic Park, the place I told my first lie not only once but several times. After a couple of pony rides, Charlie would head for the bumper cars and speedboats while I remained with the ponies, using up all my ride tickets. By the age of seven, I wanted to own a pony so badly that I told the other kids in line, "I am the owner of that beautiful palomino pony. Her name is Goldie. I just let the park use her." The kids simply shook their heads and moved closer to the entrance gate. Hey, it was my first real lie.

Back at Grandma's house, after our busy day at the park, Charlie and I pestered her to let us see yet more horses. They lived right in Grandma's backyard! We eagerly made our way down the winding stairs from the second floor of the two-family house to the cement yard for yet another thrill, gawking at the butts of six huge workhorses parked head-on in their narrow, standing-room-only stalls. We always kept our distance as the owner, on the first floor, had instructed us. Water steamed off the hot cement and off the backs of the hosed-down giants like mist off a pond. The tails of the horses swung contentedly as their unseen faces dipped into large feed buckets. The sound of munching filled us with an unexplainable peace. We loved the earthy smell of them, the presence of them, and the look of them, even if it was only the tail end.

Goldfish Adventure

During the summer of our ninth year, we made our first excursion over the Bloomfield line and discovered a large, man-made pond filled with multicolored goldfish located in the center of a circular road, and surrounded by a cluster of quaint little dwellings that looked like gingerbread houses.

On our next trip to the pond, we carried a fish net and two buckets. Heading up a hill on our way home, we resembled Jack and Jill, except our buckets were filled with water AND beautiful fish. As she did after every one of our excursions to woods or water, Mom came dutifully outside to admire our treasure. If we brought home a frog, she'd stretch out her dainty hand -- palm up, fingers flat – in fine horse-feeding fashion, and let us place the frog on her pretend lily pad. If we brought home little garter snakes, she'd put her hands behind her back and say, "That's nice."

We knew right where to find the snakes: in the sunny meadow section of the nearby woods. We'd just flip over any piece of sun-baked cardboard or wood and grab for the wiggly, brown snakes with our grubby, little hands. Next we'd drop them into an empty Quaker Oats canister, and bring them home to a big cardboard box on our open back porch … from which they'd always escape. Mom made a much bigger fuss over our colorful fish than she did over our snakes but wondered aloud how the fish would survive in the small buckets.

"We'll have to talk to Daddy tonight and see if he can come up with something from the factory," Mom said. "The area under the lilac bush beyond my vegetable garden would be a good shady location for some sort of fish pond." She was proud of our double lot and wanted the whole family to enjoy it. Dad had his chicken coop, Mom and Jean had their garden, and Charlie and I had … well, just about whatever we wanted.

The next evening, we paced back and forth in the driveway, waiting for Dad. His five o'clock arrival sent us scurrying to the big, black Packard with the swan ornament on the hood.

"Okay, okay, let me out of the car so I can get to the back door," he said, as he gingerly opened the front one and flipped his Camel cigarette onto the driveway. We jumped up and down, as if on pogo sticks, as he slid the shallow white tub off the back seat. It was as long as the width of the car and bright as snow against the blacktop.

Even though Dad always liked to have dinner the moment he arrived home from work, on that particular day, after taking one look at our buckets of floundering fish, he went right to work digging a long, six-inch deep ditch for the tub. At the end, where the drain would rest, Dad dug a deep hole for the dry well, which Charlie and I filled with stones we sifted from the mound of rocky soil. Within an hour our fish were swimming gracefully around their new home, no more floundering.

As Mom served up the reheated dinner, we all talked about the fish adventure. It soon became apparent to Charlie and me that everyone had a different definition of "pond." We realized that Mom thought the fish came from a small, natural lake, while Jean had the right idea. "Are you two talking about the big, round, cement, pond with the fountain in Halcyon Park?" she asked, while Charlie and I realized from the tone of her voice that it was not exactly a public fishing park. Perhaps not wanting to have wasted his time installing the enamel tub, Dad said nothing. Neither did we.

We enjoyed feeding bugs to our fish and watching their water ballets throughout the summer, each week running fresh water into one end of the little pond while draining the dirty water out the other end. Come early fall, we trudged back to Halcyon Park and released our beautiful treasures to the deeper water before our backyard pond froze. We emptied it for the winter and tried to imagine what we would do with it the next summer.

Twins: one boy/one girl

Mom and twins

Jean and twins

Twins graduation from Kindergarten

Halloween

Mom and Dad

The Turtle Caper

Since I've already confessed to lying about owning a pony, I may as well tell you about my intentional stealing … well, actually, I played lookout while Charlie carried out the dastardly deed I plotted.

The whole saga started with a trip to Bloomfield Pet Shop, one chilly autumn day. Dad had taken us for bird feed, and ended up giving in to our pestering for two of the little, green turtles "begging" to come home with us. On the drive back to 38 Marcy Avenue, Dad had to tell us repeatedly to calm down so he could concentrate on the road. Even with the fear of him loosing his temper, which was always an underlying threat, we had a difficult time settling down.

Arriving home safely, we ran straight to Mom with our new pets, the little kidney-shaped plastic bowl complete with a palm tree to stick in the middle of the raised island, and the container of turtle food, which consisted entirely of dried ant eggs. With the enthusiasm of a circus ringmaster, Mom helped us set it all up. Charlie and I fed our turtles every day, did daily water changes, put them on a sunny windowsill for an hour each day, and held races with them on the linoleum kitchen floor. They lasted about two months.

"But, Mom, we took … took … good care of them, and they … they … still died," we stammered between sobs. Mom enlightened us about turtle heaven and dried our tears. She helped us bury our deceased pets in the backyard garden of dead flowers and even let us use her red nail polish to paint the turtle's names on their gravestones. Timmy and Tilley were laid to rest in peace.

The next May, we turned ten and strayed farther and farther from home. One day, we met a girl named Carol who lived in the Watsessing section of Bloomfield. She brought us into her backyard, where, before my very eyes, lay her outdoor pond loaded with beautiful shiny turtles.

I stared in awe at the green ones with red cheeks, just like the ones we had lost. Sunning themselves were brown turtles with thin yellow lines in the pattern of their shells and black ones with red trim on the edges of their shells. Suddenly, they all scurried from the grassy area into the water. We laughed with delight.

"Wow," I said, "you have tons of turtles, you lucky stiff you." Then I told Carol about the two we had that died.

She smugly replied, "Actually, I have exactly thirteen slider turtles, which means they slide into the water when they are frightened. They must be kept outdoors in summer and indoors in winter, with heat lights mounted to their aquarium, but they need to be able to get away from their heat source when it gets too hot. That's why we provided them with those hollow logs. They must also be fed live food since they are carnivorous, you know. Those ant eggs the stores sell have no nutritional value whatsoever! And those stupid plastic bowls are death traps! My dad brought my turtles back from a Florida business trip last month, and we have given them the perfect home."

Well, I thought, *it looks pretty good to me except for that filthy water in that little-bitty cement pond. They need clean water you dummy.*

Her dad had actually made a pretty cool set-up for the turtles. The only problem seemed to be that there was no drain to get rid of the dirty water, like in the tub my dad had sunk in our yard the summer before to house the goldfish. *Hmmm,* I thought, *now I know what to do with our empty tub.*

We told Carol about the nice little pond we had in our yard. "It would be great for a couple of turtles," I said with enthusiasm. "I live right on the other side of the railroad tracks at the other end of the GE parking lot; you could visit them." I nagged and nagged, but she didn't give in like Dad had. I even offered my allowance. Two weeks allowance. Three weeks allowance … to be paid in installments. But she wouldn't part with even one of her thirteen turtles.

On our way home, I hatched my evil plan and explained to Charlie how easy it would be. "Carol's big shot dad is taking her and her mom to a movie tomorrow. While they're gone, you go into their yard with a bucket and take a couple, and I'll stand guard out front." I pestered and pestered until Charlie gave in. Sometimes "big brothers" don't know how to say no.

Charlie tiptoed out of Carol's back yard with a bucket of four turtles; I sent him back for more. He came back with six turtles, and I sent him back for even more. We lugged home all thirteen turtles!

As I gleefully watched *my* turtles bobbing like apples in the pristine water of my superior pond, Carol and her father stormed across the parking lot, spotted me, and stomped into our yard. I knew if I ran into the house I'd lead them straight to my father and his leather strap that was used for more than sharpening his straight razor, so I froze like petrified wood … except for the shaking. Retrieving their turtles while delivering a tongue lashing, they assured me they'd be calling the police as soon as they got back home.

I was obviously no better at stealing than I was at lying. Charlie had cautioned me about being greedy. "She won't notice if only four are missing," he'd said. But, no-o-o, I had to have them all. Evidently, an empty pond was as much a give-away as the handful of pony ride tickets I'd held at Olympic Park while pretending to be the "owner" of Goldie.

While Charlie was off playing, I spent hours at the front window of my bedroom, looking down at the street, chewing my fingernails and praying. I promised, way more than thirteen times, to never lie or steal again. As the sun went down and the gaslights came on, I finally realized the cops weren't coming. "Now I lay me down to sleep … and I promise to go to Confession on Saturday."

What Stitches? What Operation?

My only fourth-grade memory is the day Sister Rose yanked on my right ear to move me along in line. I reacted like she'd poked me with a cattle prod. "No, no!" I shrieked. "My stitches will come out." I ran off holding my hands over my ear. I huddled in the corner and inspected my hands for blood or -- worse yet -- my ear! I truly believed she could have pulled my ear off. I sobbed. Sister stared. She looked totally baffled.

But that tug on my ear had sent a crystal clear memory flooding into my brain. I could see myself running to the foot of a hospital crib to the gentle, gray-haired man who had fixed my ears. He hugged me against his snowy white coat and told me how beautiful I would look when the thick white bandages were unwrapped from my head. Then he held me at arms length and told me to be very careful not to pull the stitches out from behind my ears.

"What are you babbling about?" Sister Rose pleaded. "Stitches? What stitches?"

When she got nothing out of me but bawling, and more ranting about my ear falling off, she turned to Charlie and begged for an answer. He told her about the operation on my ears the year before kindergarten and how my head was wrapped like a swami's.

"What operation? That was years ago. Can she hear me?"

Still not understanding the wounded-animal display, she gently, very gently, led me to the principal's office where she called Mom about my bizarre behavior.

"Mrs. Merlau, this is Sister Rose. I am totally confused. I gave Dorothy's ear a tug to move her along, and she's been sobbing ever since about stitches and her ear falling off. I'm so upset. What is she talking about?"

After several minutes of listening and nodding, Sister Rose burst into laughter and assured Mom that she would tell me.

Tell me what? What's so funny? Now I was the confused one.

Sister sat me down and explained more about the surgery I'd had five years ago. "When you were born, you were cute as a button, but your ears did not lay nice and flat against your head. It reminded your father of the teasing he had received as a child, and he decided his little girl would not be called 'Big ears' or 'Elephant ears' as he had been in school. He saved the money to have your ears surgically stitched back. Now they will never stick out ... or fall off. But just to make you feel better, I promise to never pull your ear again."

The Fate of Two Frogs

One fine summer's day, Charlie and I headed to the pond at Halcyon Park to check on the goldfish we had returned the summer before. We were sure we'd recognize our old friends. The bright, sunny day of innocent adventure turned suddenly into a day of innocence lost.

As we skipped up to the pond, we noticed three boys, bigger and older than the two of us. We stopped. They huddled in a small circle. They held a frog and matches. Oh my God! They dropped lit matches down the frog's throat … and laughed. They burned his squirming feet … and laughed. Charlie and I almost threw up. We stared in horror.

"What are you looking at?" one of them snarled. We turned and ran.

Halfway home, panting and crying, we slowed down. As we trudged the rest of the way home, we kept asking each other, "Why? Why were they burning that poor little frog? Why didn't we try to stop them? Why weren't we as brave as Uncle John when he saved those kittens?" It was our last trip to Halcyon Park.

Mom tried to answer the recurring questions for us, telling us some kids were just plain mean, and we were too little to help the frog. She pointed out that we were outnumbered, and Uncle John was not. We tried to believe her reasoning but still felt mad, frustrated, and guilty.

Two days later, still depressed, my brother and I heard the voice of a frog croaking up from a storm drain at the far edge of the GE parking lot. We dropped to our knees, then onto our bellies, and scanned the shadows beneath the rusty grate for a glimpse of the desperate creature. The grate was imbedded over a drain on a level surface of lowland by the railroad tracks. The grate was a slab of rectangular openings a little larger than our hands, but the depth of the drainage well was much deeper than the length of our arms.

Even with these seemingly insurmountable obstacles, we knew we had to save the life of that frog. It had been a very hot, dry summer, and we could see only a small puddle shimmering in the bottom of the dark drain. We pondered the situation like two engineers preparing to build the Holland Tunnel.

As the sun rose higher in the sky, we tramped home for lunch. Mom cheered us on as we scribbled little diagrams and lists of possible rescue equipment. After much planning, we ran back to the frog prison holding a flashlight, two long, thin sticks, and a small paper bag. We speared through both sides of the bag near the top with one of the sticks and then spread the bag open. It became our makeshift frog net.

It took quite a while to squeeze the stick and bag carefully through one of the openings and reshape the bag with our hands straining through the grate. We carefully lowered it to the bottom and then stuck the other stick through one of the other openings. Lying on our bellies for hours, we directed the flashlight at the hopping frog while repeatedly positioning the bag in front of him, and tapping him lightly on the butt with the other stick.

While four small hands worked to save his life, the frog hopped to the left of the bag, to the right of the bag, and occasionally on top of the bag ... squashing it. We'd ease the makeshift net up and reshape the bag over, and over, and over. All the while the hot sun, that did not shed much light on the bottom of the drainage ditch, penetrated our summer clothing and bare skin. But nothing was too much effort for this frog.

After hours of labor, our plan succeeded. The frog finally hopped into the paper bag! Slowly, very slowly, we raised the stick hand over hand, until it hovered just below the grate. Since my hands were smaller than Charlie's, they became the support under the bag while his hands gently maneuvered the squirming sack through the opening.

Scurrying away from the grate, we hopped up and down with the sweet taste of victory. After releasing the frog to a marshy area on the other side of the tracks, we marched home covered with dirt, sweat, and red skin to a hero's welcome of Hostess cupcakes and ice-cold milk. Mom also promised we could call Uncle John that evening with our tale of triumph.

Santas, Dolls, and Guns

Christmases were spent at our home filled with new toys and clothes, decorations created by Dad, and sugar cookies baked by Mom. The same Feeney relatives from Easter and Thanksgiving arrived with bundles of wrapped gifts and big appetites for the identical menu as the last holiday.

Uncle Bill, who was an East Orange policeman, Aunt Kathleen, and my cousins Russell and Karen, spent their holidays with my aunt's family. Since this Feeney family lived nearby, we saw them often. I became like a big sister to Karen, who was a few years younger than I. Whenever our neighbor, Mrs. Limpert, wasn't on the party line, Mom and Aunt Kathleen took their turn gabbing on the rotary phone. Why Mom stayed standing through the entire conversation, attached to the four-foot wire as if on a leash, always baffled me. There were no portable phones back then, but the dining room chairs -- four feet away – were certainly portable.

Every Christmas, our house became a winter wonderland. Decorations on the front porch included a six-foot Santa and a revolving silver Christmas tree with blue bulbs and a color-changing spotlight shining up from beneath it. The front lawn became the stomping grounds for eight large reindeer and a red-nosed leader.

Dad was a machinist who put his mechanical skills to work not only for his own pleasure but also for the benefit of his family. Far from an affectionate man, he showed his love through deeds. Each December, he became as scarce as Santa in August. Dad disappeared to his basement workshop full of tools where he worked his magic. Mom, Jean, Charlie, and I, wrapped presents to the rhythm of buzzing and hammering coming up through the floorboards.

The humungous Santa, dressed in an extra-large red velvet suit, was the first wonder to emerge from the cellar. His fluffy white beard, mustache, and flowing hair were as soft as Suzie our rabbit. Not only was Santa big and strong and beautiful, but he actually waved. His massive arm moved back and forth, greeting all who passed our house. While they gazed at the front of our Santa, the backside of our plywood friend mesmerized my brother and me. Dad had used the workings of an old Singer sewing machine to put Santa into action.

Through the years, the famous reindeer, the familiar Nativity scene, and cherry-cheeked, mitten-clad carolers were added to the front lawn display. Each magnificent decoration made us feel very special to live in a winter wonderland.

An important part of the seasonal routine was listening to Bing Crosby's Christmas album on single 78-rpm records over and over, almost as many times as Mom tried annually to talk me into asking Santa for a doll instead of a gun. Almost as many times as Mom wailed, "When is she going to start acting like a girl?"

I think Mom's happiest Christmas occurred the year I finally agreed to ask the Santa at Bamberger's Department Store for a doll. My request for "a doll … and a gun" sent Santa's "ho ho" resounding throughout the store. Mom breathed a sigh of relief and took us to our yearly treat at Bamberger's beautiful Pine Room for lunch. I always ordered bacon, lettuce, and tomato on white toast with "plenty of mayonnaise" and a black and white soda.

Unfortunately Mom's joy on Christmas morning lasted no longer than it took me to unwrap my "Jenny" Southern Belle doll and plop her on the couch to become the target of our Roy Rogers and Dale Evans guns.

Once again the wail was heard, "When is she going to start acting like a girl?"

Year-Round Wailing

My mother's lamentations over my behavior were heard off and on throughout my entire eight years of grammar school. Like the time her boy/tomboy twins climbed the tallest backyard tree.

The split tree that shot up like a two-pronged fork and topped off above our house presented a challenge we could not resist. Each time we climbed the separate, sway-in-the-breeze trunks, the tree called to us, "Climb higher, climb higher," until the day we reached the top and realized we were looking down at our brown, shingled roof and the chimney Santa must have used every Christmas.

With our help, the tree swayed gloriously back and forth while we reached towards each other, encouraging each trunk to bend towards the other so we could grasp hands. Our feelings of joy, conquest, and sheer ecstasy must have rivaled those of the saints -- or at least mountain climbers. It felt so awesome that we wanted to share the moment with our ever-enthusiastic mom.

"Mom! Mom!" we called simultaneously at the top of our lungs from the top of the tree. After much yelling, Mom finally appeared at the second floor window at the back of the house.

"Up here! Up here!"

She stopped surveying the ground and looked higher to the low willow we often climbed. "Are you in the willow tree?" she called.

"No, no, look up higher!" we shouted with delight.

"Don't tell me you've climbed that split tree?"

"Yes, yes, look higher!" we proclaimed in unison, as if we had accomplished the dream of every Mom's heart to see her children swaying in the flimsy, top branches of a forty-foot tree.

When Mom yelled, "Get down here this minute," after spotting us, we knew we had made another big mistake. We grumbled all the way down the tree, all the way across the yard, and all the way up the stairs to our rooms where we spent the rest of the day. Although she was certainly upset over the possible danger to her little boy, she wailed again over the jeopardy her little girl had placed herself in. "When will you start acting like a girl?"

Big sister, Jean, asked the same question every time she brushed the knots out of the long hair I insisted on keeping, but not brushing. To keep me sitting long enough to accomplish the challenging task, Jean made up little jingles like, "Knotty, knotty please come out." She was like a second Mom.

One hot summer day, Dad, who worked for Thomas Toy Manufacturing Company, came home late from overtime with a pair of plastic water rifles for his young twins. We were ecstatic but had to wait until morning to actually fill them with water. The next day, Mom enjoyed watching us run around the yard, spraying each other with cool water. Each time we "accidentally" sprayed her, we were rewarded with her laughter -- delightful as the sound of wind chimes. On day two of our water war, Mom went back to her housework, and Charlie and I played hide-seek-and-spray in the yard again till lunchtime.

After our Becker's milk and egg salad on Wonder Bread, our water fight continued and overflowed into the GE parking lot. The employees' cars quickly became black mountains to hide behind and ambush each other for hours, returning occasionally to our backyard hose for reloading.

As the tired, hot, factory workers trudged to their cars, rolled down their windows, started their engines, and headed home through the single-file exit road, they joked with us and laughed at our game ... giving us a brilliant idea. We ran to opposite sides of the narrow road and ambushed the drivers as they passed by; they loved it -- at least the first dozen or so. They kidded with us about the much-needed showers we were providing.

Much to our surprise, Scrooge showed up in the middle of summer. He stormed out of his car, screaming and cursing, and chased us all the way across the parking lot to the trees and bushes along the railroad tracks, where we finally lost him. Flat on our stomachs, we trembled in the underbrush, gasping for air. We remained hidden; clinging to our rifles for what seemed like eternity, until we were absolutely sure the angry factory worker had left. We slunk home by way of tree-filled backyards along the edge of the parking lot. Still trembling, we dashed across the corner of the parking lot onto our property.

As we slouched at the dinner table, wordlessly pushing Mom's famous meatloaf around our plates, she gave us her notorious sad-eye look and silent treatment. Jean chatted on and on about her new boyfriend, and Dad bragged about the machine he repaired that no one else could fix. Mom, Charlie, and I sat in silence. Mom knew by our sullen behavior that we had been up to no good, suspecting it had to do with our new weapons. She simmered in her skepticism, while Charlie and I stewed in our contrition. She never questioned us or mentioned her suspicion to Dad, who would have used the strap on *our* bottoms to get to *the* bottom of our mysterious behavior. Instead, our water rifles disappeared for two weeks while Mom lamented.

Then there was the time our neighbor, Greg, had the nerve to call us "The Merlau Brats" right in our own backyard! I picked up the nearest stick and chased him all the way to his front door. It must have been a weekend because Dad was home and saw the whole thing. He and my brother laughed uproariously and slapped me on the back. Mom sent me to my room. This time, with my ear pressed to the door, I could hear a response to her moaning and groaning.

"Stop worrying about her," Dad said. "My sister was a tomboy growing up with me and Art, and look at what a good wife and mother she turned out to be. Elsie started acting like a girl when she went to high school. Dotty will be fine."

Dungaree Aunt and
The Hardy Boys

My father's prediction about my behavior got me thinking about my Aunt Elsie. Although I never saw her in anything but dungarees, she was as sweet and loving as my dress-wearing aunts. She lived in Waretown, New Jersey, near Barnegat Bay with my Uncle Al and my three cousins: Robert, Russell, and Ronny ... the Hardy Boys.

Our family traveled down to the shore several times each summer. The other four members of my family loved the early morning drive; I hated it. I always got carsick. Although Jean tried distracting me by pointing out the tin soda-bottle signs and other landmarks along Route 9, and Charlie told jokes, I remained queasy for most of the two-and-a-half-hour trip. With the smell of salt air and the appearance of the big green dinosaur statue in Bayville, I perked up, knowing my ordeal was almost over. The split-rail fence along Finnegan's Farm, adjacent to Oyster Creek, made me smile because our destination was right around the corner.

The first form of entertainment at the Hardy's house came from rocks: rocks of all sizes, shapes, and colors. The Hardys were rock hunters and filled their basement and backyard workshop with the specimens they gathered on numerous camping trips. Shelves and windowsills glittered with rose quartz, green agate, and purple amethyst.

Tumblers in their workshop made a delightful racket as they turned some other rocks into beautiful, smooth, semi-precious gems. To this day, I have a brooch given to me by Aunt Elsie during my high school years. It is in the form of a painter's pallet, and the tiny stones create the dabs of color ready for the gold brush that lies across the pallet.

After the initial excitement at the Hardy residence, it would be time to scoot next door for a visit with Grandma and Grandpa Merlau. While digging into milk and gingerbread cookies, we asked Grandma and Grandpa questions about Germany and Paterson, New Jersey, where they raised their three children: my father, Charles, my Uncle Art, and my Aunt Elsie. On each outing to Waretown, we learned how to pronounce a few more German words, but we never learned how to spell any of them.

Since Grandma's small Waretown house was full of valuable knick-knacks, and children are full of energy, we kids would all return to the Hardys' large lot where Bobby, Russell, Charlie, and I hauled out the beat up baseball equipment from the garage for a game. Jean, being the oldest -- and a girl who acted like one -- showed no interest in the game. She spent her time playing with little Ronny, the youngest of us all. Since there were only four players, the game consisted of a batter and pitcher on one team and two outfielders on the other, who tried to tag the runner out. While Charlie pitched to me, Bob and Russ played the outfield. After three outs, our cousins got to pitch and bat.

Hunger or summer heat ended the game and sent the players trudging into the bungalow to flop on the Colonial style couch and chairs in the cozy living room. While waiting for Aunt Elsie, Mom, and Jean to put the finishing touches on the spread of cold cuts, homemade breads, and salads, Uncle Al picked up his guitar and entertained us with country and western songs like Mom's favorite, Tennessee Waltz.

I still have a special fondness for my, now deceased, Aunt Elsie who also started her life as a tomboy, never gave up her dungarees, married, and raised three boys. My life has been cut from the same cloth: tomboy, married, three boys, but my denim pants are called jeans.

Motorcycle Uncle and His Shore Family

Uncle Art, my Dad's younger brother, Aunt Millicent, Virginia, and Arthur Jr. lived right around the corner from the other shore relatives and were on the agenda for a late afternoon visit. Virginia, close to Jean in age, provided her with a peer, while Charlie and I played with our younger cousin, Arthur.

Aunt Millicent, who always had the most wonderful laugh, was the last relative from her generation and the preceding one to leave this world. She died in 2009 after 95 active years. She worked as a waitress at Captain's Inn in Forked River for twenty-five years, and Uncle Art worked there for about ten as a bartender. Back then; when the Captain's Inn closed for the winter, and cousin Arthur was stationed at Barbers Point Naval Air Station in Hawaii, my aunt and uncle took extensive, well-earned vacations in the Aloha state.

At their Waretown house, Aunt Millicent had provided us with chocolates and other sweets, while we talked -- under Uncle Art's supervision -- to English speaking people around the world on his ham radio. Although that international adventure amazed us, Charlie and I much preferred the adventures we had with Uncle Art on the motorcycle he owned when they lived up in Roselle. Arthur was just a baby then, and Jean and Virginia much too feminine, but, of course, a motorcycle was right up the twins' alley. Although the rides consisted of trips around the block at 15-20 MPH, to us they felt like rip-roaring, hair-blowing, cross-country races. On one occasion, our enthusiasm got the best of Jean; she actually broke down and went for a spin. Once.

In Waretown, while Jean and Virginia chatted about movie stars and boys, Arthur brought Charlie and me to the outside cinder block shower stall where we attempted the impossible: trying to catch the small, light brown lizards that scurried frantically all over the block walls. Sometimes we left Arthur in the yard he was not allowed to vacate while we fought our way through the sticker bushes and evergreens of the Pine Barrens to a little tributary of Oyster Creek, where we flipped rocks over in search of salamanders. I'm not sure if we ever found any of them, but I know we never caught any because if we had, they would have been brought home and housed in some sort of habitat of Dad's making.

What I do remember us bringing home from the shore were two box turtles, which ended up housed in the "turtle run" Dad constructed of railroad ties. Over night the number of turtles dropped to one. It took us a while to realize that the remaining turtle had served as a stepstool for the escapee. The lone turtle thrived on lettuce and the slugs we tracked down and speared for him.

Dad always tried to start home from Waretown before dark to avoid the deer that grazed at sunset … and sometimes ran in front of cars. We usually made it halfway home before darkness filled the skies, and the Sandman filled the children's eyes. The childhood trip from my house in East Orange to Waretown, which took well over two hours, now takes five minutes since I retired to the town-next-door called Forked River.

Impressions of Sister Francis

Our seventh grade teacher was Sister Francis. I loved her; she was the sweetest, most gentle nun in the entire school. Charlie saw her more like the Grim Reaper.

I had become one of those "yucky" older kids who formed smoking circles in Watsessing Park. I had started hanging around with, Mary, a girl who transferred from Ampere, a tougher section of town. It was inevitable that someone would squeal on us. I don't know what happened to her, but I was devastated by my punishment.

Sister Francis didn't say a word. She just kept giving me the same silent treatment and same sad-eyed look Mom had perfected. Sister was even better at it. I stopped smoking ... at least until I entered high school.

Another day, Charlie and his best friend, Jimmy, kept turning toward me from their front row seats and making the goofiest faces imaginable. Every time Sister Francis turned to write on the blackboard, they swung around and blocked my line of vision with a variety of funny faces. Since I sat in the second row, right behind the two comedians, their antics were as impossible to ignore as the laughter percolating within me.

Charlie and Jimmy's timing rivaled that of Burns and Allen. The instant our teacher began writing on the blackboard, they swiveled towards me and continued their routine as smoothly as the comedians on our 14-inch DuMont after a television commercial. With each silly face, my stifled laughter bubbled closer to the surface until escaping my lips in subdued chuckles, and finally exploding into uproarious laughter. Sister turned, and gave me that look of disappointment. "Dorothy, go stand in the hallway until you get control of yourself."

Okay, I thought, *I can do this.* I stood in the hall taking deep breaths, and beseeching the saints whose pictures lined the wall. I imagined Sister Francis finally losing it with me, as she had with others, and smacking *me.* That thought did the trick; I felt ready to return to the classroom just as Sister Catherine came marching down the hall with her class in tow. Since it was a hot, June day, she was leading them to the water fountain, like sheep to a trough.

"And just what are you doing out here?" she asked in a suspicious tone.

As I explained my situation to Sister Catherine, her students experienced the same scenario I had just gone through: bubbling laughter, escaping chuckles, and finally exploding hilarity. It took numerous reprimands from Sister Catherine to move her class through the water fountain routine and back to their classroom, and several more minutes before I considered myself under control. Wrong! Upon entering the classroom, I lost it again … and again … and again. After many trips to the hallway, I finally made it back to my seat … and never got smacked.

Which brings me to the reason Charlie had a different impression of Sister Francis. It seems that she was one of the instigators in putting an end to the class plays because "certain people" were always stars, while "others" had lesser parts. That just wasn't "charitable." Dance recitals were more equitable. Since Charlie always had a staring role in the class plays, this did not sit well with him. But he went along with the dance recital routine.

The evening of the show we were all dressed in our Sunday best, lined up with our designated partners, and prepared to take our places on the stage before the curtain was drawn. Charlie gave his best come-hither stare to the high school girl who had taught us the dance steps, and, SLAM, he got it across the face. Not from the girl, but from Sister Francis.

We all scurried to our places on stage and waited for the phonograph needle to drop on Glenn Miller's *String of Pearls.* The curtain opened to a bunch of giggling pre-teens trying not to sink into fits of laughter as they stared at my poor brother. His partner whispered in his ear about the big red hand impression on his left cheek, while the rest of his face turned crimson.

A Birthday Party of Horror and Ecstasy

For our twelfth birthday party, Mom had invited the entire seventh grade class, believing the warm, May weather, along with the badminton and croquet games set up on our grassy double lot, would keep the twenty-some kids out of trouble. But she had never met Matt, the class tough guy, or imagined that Ralph, the bully from next door, would crash our party looking for trouble. Ralph, a couple of years older than us, had been terrorizing the neighborhood for years.

Once, when I was around eight, Ralph had tied me up and stuffed my mouth full of mud and stones ... for no reason. He left me crying and choking in my own driveway for what seemed like hours, until Charlie found me. As he struggled with the knots, he ranted and raved about how he was "Gonna get that bum." I don't know how my big brother accomplished it, but Ralph never bothered me again.

At our party, Matt, who lived to fight, turned out to be more than a match for Ralph. While the two of them went at it like Rocky Graziano and Tony Zale, the other boys gathered around to watch and cheer. The girls formed a circle away from the brawl, where they cringed and cried, and -- miracle of miracles -- I joined them!

The look of horror on Mom's face as she broke up the fight by threatening to call the police, misted into one of ecstasy as she gazed at her tomboy in a circle of girls. She looked like she was having the religious experience of her lifetime: the canonization of her very own Saint Dorothy. Too bad it was only a foreshadowing of the conversion whose time had not yet come.

Ghost Houses and High Girders

During the later years of grammar school, the construction of the Garden State Parkway provided us with oodles of opportunities for adventure. The empty houses of those who had to relocate begged to be investigated, and we became the willing investigators. There was no "trashing" in those days, just a simple jimmying of windows until they rose high enough for us to squeeze into the forbidden rooms.

The first house we explored had belonged to the Kellys. Once the window was opened, we slipped in over the windowsill, dust-filled sunlight at our backs casting eerie shadows across the hardwood floors and empty walls. As we waited for our eyes to adjust to the interior darkness -- and our nerves to adjusted to the latest test we were about to put them through -- we stood in creepy stillness. Slowly, we made out the frame marks where the Norman Rockwells had hung. Next we were able to see the light strings hanging from the lifeless ceiling fixtures and the deep footprints left by the bulky green couch.

Eventually, our strengthening nerves pushed us farther into the empty interior, every sound echoing and making us jump out of our Keds. Just as the sun began to set, we ended up in the second floor bedroom where Kevin's grandmother had died. We looked at each other with saucer eyes and whispered, "ghost." With goose bumps on our backs we tiptoed down the stairs and out the window.

Another adventure provided by the construction of the Garden State Parkway was the girders that stretched high over the railroad tracks. These reddish-colored I-beams connected the hills built up on each side of the tracks. They were intended to support a bridge for the steady flow of Parkway traffic, but to us they were intended for a high-wire act under a big top of blue sky.

Being the lovers of heights that we were, the I-beams presented a challenge we could no more resist than tall trees. There was a set of two girders every few feet; each set consisting of a higher and a lower one. As we looked down at the glistening tracks below, we inched our feet along the lower girder, with one hand extended for balance and the other hand moving along the higher girder, until we reached the other side.

Although those "hand rails" made us feel quite secure, we still prayed that no train would roar under us as we performed our high wire act. But mostly, we prayed that Mom never got wind of those escapades.

A Whale of a Tale

Once the Parkway was completed, and we were still alive, the access road made it much easier to get to the mysterious Clifford J. Scott High School for a self-guided tour. We weren't supposed to set our feet in that door for another year, but in that summer between seventh and eighth grades, we could wait no longer.

We jogged the two blocks along the access road to the public high school we would be attending after graduation from Holy Name. At first, we were just anxious for a better look at the outside of the ominous red brick building with the huge white columns flanking the double-door entry. But when we got there, we just stood staring at the front of the menacing building like a couple of prisoners on our way to the big house. It seemed so overwhelming compared to our much smaller grammar school. Slowly we made our way around it until we were at its back wall. Seeing no one else around, we squeezed behind the tall shrubs, stood on tiptoe, and peeked in the window. The cavernous classroom yawned at us like the jaws of a whale, a whale that became as irresistible as the empty houses along the Parkway had been.

Coming full-circle back to the front entrance, we tried the door. It was locked. Looking up, we spotted an open window above the doorway – decision time. One glance at each other, and, before we could say "stupid," the decision was made.

Using the pillar to his left and the brick wall to his right, Charlie scurried up to the overhang and in through the window. Once inside, he hurried down the nearest stairway and let me in the front door. Trembling, we stared at the walls of closed, gray lockers, and bare classroom doors along the corridors. No holy pictures, no brightly colored student drawings ... no reason to ever want to go there.

But we sure found reason to get the heck out of there when we heard a door squeak open and the sudden burst of adult voices. "Teachers," we whispered as we flew out the front door like Jonah spewed from the mouth of the whale.

The Belly of the Whale and Beyond

Clifford J. Scott High School was as consuming as we had expected. Charlie and I were no longer together in the same classroom for the whole day. We had separate schedules for different classes; I was in the business course and Charlie in college prep.

As we sat at our dining room table doing our first night's homework, Charlie and I compared our schedules. I shook my head. "Where is room 121?" I asked. "When I turn the bend, the numbers go crazy. Where is the principal's office? I was sent there today and couldn't find it. Why can't we have even one stinking class together?"

For me, the first week felt like Eddie Robinson's Halloween basement all over again, only without my brother to lean on. I roamed through the maze of hallways as though blinded by cobwebs. I never knew what I was going to run into: rowdy boys, scary teachers, or, worst of all, big-mouthed, big-breasted, big-shot girls.

Those lockers we had spotted in the belly of the whale became fodder for new nightmares. Fear of forgetting combinations still shows up in my twenty-first century dreams. Was it 23 – 47 – 32 or 32 – 47 – 23? As the homeroom bell blared, I trembled over the locker dial … was it right, left, right, or left, right, left?

On the rare occasions I was first into a classroom, it felt as eerie as those empty houses along the Parkway, but instead of darkness, my eyes had trouble adjusting to the bright fluorescent lights. Where was everyone? As other students entered, relief enveloped me. I finally came to appreciate the girls from Holy Name: Maureen, Joyce, and Patty became my guides into the world of other people.

Always the target of class clowns, I was learning that in high school laughing or talking in class did not bring down the wrath of God, or -- in my case -- standing in the hallway, like at Holy Name, but rather a trip to the principal's office and detention. Repetition is a good teacher; before long I could walk there with my eyes closed. The up side was it made me more familiar with the layout of the interior.

Charlie quickly discovered all the new girls. And I discovered the cutest boy in the world. I ran home from the freshman dance to tell Mom about the handsome redheaded boy I'd danced with.

"Oh, Mom, he's so nice and danced with only me. Can I go to the football game next week? He said he was going. It's an away game and a bus will take us. I have to find out his name. Some of the kids from Holy Name are going. Please. Please."

"Does your brother want to go?"

"I don't know. I don't care. I'll be safe. Miss Black is going. She's my stenography teacher. She's real nice and pretty. The boys call her 'legs.'"

"Legs?" said Mom.

"Um, well, only some of the boys call her that. Mostly the football players, and they'll be on a different bus. Oh, Mom, please, I want to see the redheaded boy again. *He* doesn't call her that.

"Well, okay, as long as you stay with the group. I'm glad to see you're gaining some independence from Charlie. It's good for both of you to discover there are other people in the world." Her dream was coming true; I was finally acting like a girl!

On the bus, Flo, a gal from my neighborhood who had gone to Franklin Public School, formally introduced me to my heartthrob, "Dot, this is Carl. Carl, this is Dot."

My heart leapt like a cheerleader; I knew his name, hip-hip-hurray! Flo had been one of his grammar school classmates, and now she was my new best friend. Flo and I sat right in front of him and his buddy and chatted all the way to the game. Carl and I stayed together at the game and every game, dance, and social event for the next four years.

Seven years after our freshman dance, I married that handsome redheaded boy, who still holds my heart in the palm of his hand. His full head of hair is as red as ever, and his memory of the pink sweater I wore at the freshman dance is crystal clear.

Dreams Come True

They say high school romances never last, but they're wrong. Not only can they last, they can improve through the years like good wine. The ingredients are: "faith, hope, and love, and the greatest of these is love." 1st Cor.13:13. We had faith in God, hope for our marriage, and love that knew how to work hard … and stay romantic.

Ten months -- and nineteen hours -- after we tied the knot, Doctor Degnan tied the knot on Drew's umbilical cord. The lengthly delivery was forgotten the minute I held my towheaded, 7 lb. 3 oz. son in my arms. Carl and I were awestruck by the first fruit of our love. Nightly feedings were never a chore; singing lullabies while brushing Drew's hair into those kewpie doll curls on top of his head became part of my 2:00AM routine.

Seventeen months after the birth of Drew, David arrived with a head full of auburn hair. He was another good-sized baby for my small frame, but all went well. It was an easier delivery. Before I knew it, he was taking his first steps in his royal blue corduroy overalls with feet and little white rubber soles.

Four years after David's arrival, Doctor Degnan predicted I was carrying "a little girl." I thought a girl would be nice until my easiest birth of all produced a 9 lb. 7 oz. linebacker. He was as beautiful as a month-old baby with smooth chubby cheeks, not a wrinkle to be found. Raising Danny was as easy as delivering him.

Carl and I got to live our own version of *My Three Sons.* The 60's TV show had no mom, but our version included one, and I was privileged to play the role. Raising my three sons gave me as much delightful stress as I hope my mom's perfect girl and her "impossible twins" gave her. Carl's career in the printing field supported us in as fine a fashion as the aeronautical engineer dad, played by Fred McMurray, in that show.

More Horse Tales and Fairy Tale Endings

Unlike the process of finding the one-and-only man of my life at age fourteen, my pursuit of the perfect horse at age forty-five did not go smoothly. Hondo, my first horse, was a gentle, beautiful, black gelding, but at seventeen hands (5'8" at the shoulders) he was way too tall for my 5'2" frame. I grew tired of mounting him via the mounting block or makeshift ladders.

Next came fifteen-hand Lady who kicked the crap out of me. She was traded to a trainer for fourteen-hand, Naomi, who threw me into a split rail fence, breaking my coccyx bone. Lady was obviously no lady, and Naomi did not live up to her kindhearted, biblical namesake.

I continued going from one horse to another in search of the perfect gelding (no more mares) and switching stables in search of longer, more challenging trails. Although none of the horses seemed to live up to Olympic Park Goldie, my first horse … oops … you know … the one I *said* was mine, I thoroughly enjoyed my fifteen-year adventure and all the wonderful horse-lovers I met. There's nothing quite like galloping along woodland trails for a rush of well-being.

I sold my last mount when I hit sixty and retirement from library work. Although I suddenly had plenty of time to ride, my small pension could not cover the rising cost of boarding, farriers, and vets. Driving past wooded areas still stirs up colorful memories, especially on crisp autumn days.

But, life goes on. I spend a good part of it listening to the purr of my cat while I stroke his back. He lies contentedly on my lap, while I gaze at my (legally owned) turtle gliding through the pristine water of his large, well-lit, and filtered aquarium. My mind drifts as I contemplate the full life I've lived and the life still to come. On nice days I can be found next to my fish pond reading a good book while listening to the fountain or walking park trails on my own two feet.

Carl and I love living on the water, on an actual island, and vacationing in Florida where my sister, her husband Paul, and most of their children live. Quality time is spent with Drew, Dave, and Dan and their growing circle of family and friends. I can almost hear Dad's spirit whispering to Mom's, "I told you, Dotty would be fine."

A few years after high school graduation, Charlie moved to California, put himself through college, became Chuck, and met the love of his life. He and his beautiful, gracious Philippino wife, Ofie, settled in San Diego. After Chuck's retirement from Federal Immigration Services and Ofie's from accounting, they moved to Las Vegas.

Our visits with them at both places, other vacationlands like Bermuda, and having them to our little house on the water for boating vacations, have been awesome. Thanks to love, phones, planes and a sense of adventure, my "big-brother" and I remain close and retain a spark of those "impossible twins."